Dearest Sarah,

All the best

[signature]

27/02/2019.

A JOURNEY FROM ME TO YOU

AISHA CAHN

My practice as a painter has become a journey for enquiry. In recent years, the curiosity of the essence of existence and the elements of nature have intrigued me, which has led me to explore the purpose of life and the Omnipresent.

ACKNOWLEDGEMENTS

I dedicate this book to my beloved late grandmother, Zuleikha Ismailjee, and my beloved late parents, Amin Hashim Patel and Gulrukhsar Amin Patel, for their unconditional love and affection and for instilling the moral and spiritual values that have made me the human being I am today. Also to my beautiful daughters, Jemma-Lia and Hanah, whom I have enjoyed giving birth to and nurturing into two fine young ladies who are my rocks and my angels.

I would also like to thank my friends and family, particularly those who encouraged me to write this book, and through whom I have learned a great deal. It's these real-life experiences that have shaped the framework of my perspective on life.

Most of all, I acknowledge the fact that I am eternally grateful to the Almighty God for creating this wonderful world I have the pleasure of exploring and being part of.

INTRODUCTION

During the past ten years of my life, I have been through some of the most poignant, emotional, and life-changing experiences. Some of them have been challenging; others have made me look at life from a positive and spiritual perspective. This journey has led me to the quest for answers to curiosity about my existence in this world and the purpose of life.

I was born into a Muslim family, which automatically made me Muslim. It wasn't through choice but by default. None of us are born into a religion through choice. It is the religion of our fathers and forefathers who instil in us a limited understanding of their faith, or in some cases, not to believe in any religion or even in God.

Most of the world's religions believe in the one universal God. However, for me to search for the answers to my quest, I began to research the Quran first, as I was told this was my guidance through life. To my astonishment, all the answers to my curiosity were revealed and explained in the Quran. I discovered that Islam is the complete religion of the three Abrahamic religions, including Judaism and Christianity. I must believe in Jesus, Moses and Mohammed (peace be upon them all) as prophets and messengers of God and in all their holy scriptures: The Torah, The Bible, and The Quran. I was to discover that apart from God creating the universe in six days, as mentioned in the Genesis, the Quran further explains this remarkable, beautiful, and perfect creation with reference to science.

I was overjoyed at these discoveries and inspired to further explore these notions through my work as an artist, bringing together the disciplines of faith and science through the form of contemporary, conceptual art. Art and science, faith and science have been interlinked for centuries, yet there seems to be a myth about their unity. For me, this unity exists, as there is an element of spirituality in each of these three disciplines which is reflected in my work.

The mysteries of existence and my own life's knowns and unknowns have shaped the framework of understanding my role in the greater landscape of this world. It has led me to become more spiritual by focussing on my inner self, which has enhanced my undying love for the Almighty God. I have become more concerned about the less fortunate and needy. I very much appreciate being born a Muslim and to share this journey with you, my fellow human beings.

Balboa Press books may be ordered through booksellers or by contacting:

Balboa Press
A Division of Hay House
1663 Liberty Drive
Bloomington, IN 47403
www.balboapress.com
1 (877) 407-4847

Because of the dynamic nature of the Internet, any web addresses or links contained in this book may have changed since publication and may no longer be valid. The views expressed in this work are solely those of the author and do not necessarily reflect the views of the publisher, and the publisher hereby disclaims any responsibility for them.

This book is a work of non-fiction. Unless otherwise noted, the author and the publisher make no explicit guarantees as to the accuracy of the information contained in this book and in some cases, names of people and places have been altered to protect their privacy.

ISBN: 978-1-5043-9538-0 (sc)
ISBN: 978-1-5043-9539-7 (e)

Library of Congress Control Number: 2018900242

Interior Graphics/Art Credit
Aisha Cahn

Print information available on the last page.

Balboa Press rev. date: 03/20/2018

BALBOA.
PRESS
A DIVISION OF HAY HOUSE

Contents

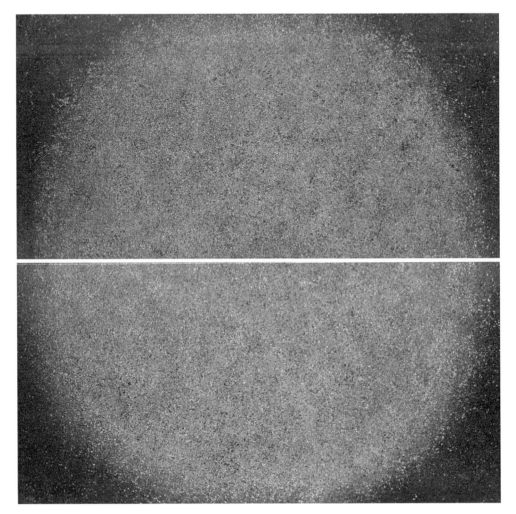

Big Bang, oil on canvas, 2013, by Aisha Cahn.

CHAPTER 1
THE GENESIS OF THINGS

I had the most inspirational afternoon today with two very dear friends of mine, Professor Modjtaba Sadria and Charlotte Rayani, from the Agha Khan University. It was a very touching moment for me, because I thought we were meeting just to catch up. We hadn't seen each other since the private viewing of my art exhibition in November 2008. However, both Charlotte and Modjtaba thought otherwise. They wanted to talk about me.

Charlotte wanted to collaborate with ING Bank to host an art exhibition in my honour the following year. Modjtaba, however, had a completely different idea in mind. He urged me to write and publish a book as a result of reading my MA Degree Fine Art dissertation, titled 'The Existence of God, the Creator of the Universe', which I gave him earlier in the month. He was impressed with the content and stated that as he was reading it, he could sense my passion about the subject matter.

I had to write a dissertation from an extremely subjective point of view. I am a practicing Muslim, with a steadfast belief in God, but I had to allow the reader to make up his or her mind as to the existence of The Almighty. It was an incredibly vast topic to research and write about, with the subject having several controversial, contentious and debatable elements to it. Professor Modjtaba found the work amusing at times, especially when I quoted philosophers', scientists', and atheists' opinions and notions on God's non-existence. By putting forward philosophies of other religions and theories attempting to justify God's existence, I created a debate on a topic I needed no convincing of.

I have had a strong belief in Allah, The Almighty, from a very young age. I was brought up in a Muslim family with a reasonable understanding of the Islamic faith. My paternal grandmother taught my four siblings and me how to pray five times a day, recite the Quran in Arabic, and other important Islamic values, similar to the ones my parents brought me up with. In Islam, there are some very special nights dedicated to prayer, remembrance and the worship of Allah. To this day, I remember the evenings when all of us – children, our parents, and grandmother – came together after dinner to pray. It was on such special nights that my parents spoke to us about the importance of our religion, the sacred nights and religious and moral values.

Moments like these, spent together as a family, made me realise that religion is not just about ritual practices and other minutiae. It is ultimately about your entire make-up as an individual – your outlook on life, your relationships with fellow human beings and the care you give to one another – all of which begins with family life.

Being an adult, I now appreciate that religious and moral values learned during childhood, stay with you throughout your existence. They help you develop into a person who is aware that life is not just about you as an individual, but as part of a community of the human race. We were brought into this world to consider our fellow human beings and to look out for those who are less fortunate than ourselves.

I didn't really understand the Quran, although I had read it several times as a child in Arabic. My grandmother believed it was important to be able to read the Holy Book in the language in which it was revealed to the Prophet Mohammed (PBUH). All we required for our belief was blind faith in Allah and in our religion.

I later realised that most people are born into a religion without choice. Our parents raise us in their beliefs and bring us up according to their limited understanding and knowledge of their faith. As I stated earlier, it is often the religion of our fathers and our forefathers that we grow into and embrace. I am a classic example of such a belief system. My grandmother dutifully taught me about my religion without me truly gaining a clear understanding of what it really meant. It was the ultimate expression of blind faith.

Faith, as I understand it, is a belief that is not based on proof of God and revelations. It is a form of loyalty which comes from within the inner self that enables a person to achieve mystical, intellectual, and emotional harmony with God and His creation. Since it is impossible to prove the existence of God with absolute certainty, one relies on one's faith. It requires no proof as this comes from the spirit within your heart.

I never gave this much thought until a recent visit to an exhibition by Ali Omar Ermes, a Lebanese artist based in London. Ermes's paintings consisted of Arabic writing, with large single letters of the alphabet in the foreground and smaller, Arabic calligraphic text in the background. They depicted the heritage of the Arabic language and Middle Eastern culture, and its adopted religion, Islam. Much of the text was poetry or prose written by renowned Middle Eastern poets and philosophers.

The exhibition was an extremely thought-provoking experience for me. It inspired me to enquire about my own heritage. It wasn't my ethnic roots or cultural background that I found myself wondering about, but instead, my origin as a human being from the beginning of time. It made me curious about the purpose of life, the creation of the universe, and the existence of God.

I never once questioned the existence of God as I was growing up. There was enough proof all around me to know He existed, and there was something more superior and intelligent than could be comprehended by the human mind. This force was responsible for the creation of this beautiful, magical, and perfectly coordinated universe.

I was astonished at the affect this exhibition had on me. I suppose there is always a turning point in one's life that makes an individual see life from a different perspective. While I loved reading the translation of some of the poetry about Middle Eastern culture and heritage, I wanted to look at the heritage of humankind as a whole, right from the year dot. I had a basic understanding of the universe being created in six days, as mentioned in the Genesis and the Quran, but what did that mean?

In an article in the *Observer* in 1954, Arnold Toynbee (1889–1975), who studied the history of humans through the ages, stated, "I have come back at the belief that religion holds the key to the mystery of existence."

I wanted to know more about this creation, this mystery of existence. I began to research by firstly attempting to understand the religion I was born into, to find the answers to my curiosity in the Quran, and if I wasn't satisfied with this form of research, I would seek the answers by researching other religious and scientific theories.

To begin this quest for knowledge, I required a starting point: reading a translation of the Holy Quran in English by Yusuf Ali. It was difficult to understand the translation as it was written in old English biblical language. In addition, the Arabic language is not very easy to translate literally; it's a very meticulous language with great emphasis on grammar. This translation, at times, leaves much to the reader's assumptions and interpretations.

After reading this translation of the Quran, I wanted to know more about these revelations sent to Prophet Mohammed (PBUH) by fully understanding the meaning and rationale behind them. I read

Shaikh Abul A'la Maududi's *The Meaning of the Quran,* with full translation and commentary written in simple, clear, and effective modern English. This comprised an edition of six volumes, which my beloved late mother had given me and which took me a few years to complete. It was beautifully translated and written with such extensive explanations of the chapters and verses of the Quran, putting everything in context. It simplified the understanding of the Quran into three categories:-

The subject matter - It is a Guidance to Man; the central theme.

The true reality - declared by God to Adam and the subsequent Messengers, and any misconceptions, theories, and contradictions to this reality about the existence of the One God, the universe, humankind and his relations with God are wrong.

The aim and object - through the revelations invited humankind to understand The Lord of the Universe, its Creator, Master, and Sovereign created us and bestowed upon us the faculties of learning, speaking, understanding, and discerning right from wrong and good from evil.

He gave humankind freedom of choice and a kind of autonomy. He instructed humankind to live on earth in accordance with His guidance.

However, even though I was now gaining a good understanding of my faith and discovering most of the answers to my quest, I was still dissatisfied. I felt that I should be reading and understanding the Quran in the language in which it was revealed. I felt handicapped and thus, frustrated because I could see on the surface that there were answers to my questions, but they were hidden beneath a cloud of precise Arabic language, I could not fully comprehend. This led me to seeking further knowledge of the Arabic language.

I ultimately appointed an Arabic tutor, Mrs Nora Bashir, who began teaching me the Arabic language, which proved to be an extremely challenging feat. Not only did I learn Arabic as a language, I also learnt about the history of Islam, the stories of the prophets and the philosophy of understanding Islam as a way of life. I used to love my sessions with her. I encouraged my daughters to join in these sessions with me, as I wanted them to have a good understanding of the religion they were born into from a professional Islamic teacher, not through the limited knowledge I had of my faith.

She came twice a week for two hourly sessions. We covered every aspect of understanding why Islam is the complete religion of the three Abrahamic religions. For example, Moses is mentioned 135 times in the Quran, Abraham 67 times, Jesus 25 times, and Mohammed only 6 times (because God was talking to him about the other prophets). Combined with the English translations and commentary, and my grasp of the Arabic language, I now had a much better understanding of the Quran. I was genuinely surprised and utterly overwhelmed to find the answers to all my questions were indeed in this Holy Book. I was surprised at how much I had discovered, far more than what my little mind had searched for.

I learnt that one-third of the Quran comprises of the other two Abrahamic religions, Christianity and Judaism. The remaining two-thirds of the Quran is about the Oneness of Allah, Prophet Mohammed (PBUH) being the last Prophet and Messenger of Islam, the Hereafter, and how God created the universe with reference to science. There are 114 chapters in the Quran. They include, "The Israelites," "Abraham," "Mary," "The Prophets," "The Romans," "The Resurrection," "The Expansion of the Universe," and "The Sure Truth." These are just some examples of how the Quran encompasses the religions of Judaism and Christianity and the expanse of the universe within it.

What fascinated me was the way the Quran explained how God created the universe with reference to science. The Quran explains the beginning of creation as, "Do not the unbelievers see that the heavens and the earth were joined together (as one unit of Creation), before We clove them asunder?" (Quran 21:30). It goes on to explain this as an explosion of smokey, gaseous matter. Then He rose over (Istawa), towards the heaven, when it was smoke and said to it and to the earth, "Come both of you willingly or unwillingly" (Quran 41:11).

By heaven is meant the whole universe. In other words, turning to the heaven means that Allah turned to the creation of the universe. Smoke implies the initial and primary stage of matter, in which it lay diffused in space in a shapeless, dust-like condition before the formation of the universe. Scientists of the modern age describe the same thing as nebulae; that is, before creation, the matter of which the universe was built lay diffused in smoke-like nebulous form.

Astronomers have recently found gas clouds in the distant Universe. Some of them are around 12 or 13 billion years old. As the Big Bang theory predicts, these ancient gas clouds are made of very different stuff to the modern universe. Most of the chemical elements in the modern universe are made inside stars. Because the gas clouds come from a time before stars, they consist almost entirely of the most basic elements, hydrogen and helium. (BBC iWonder)

The concept of the Big Bang was a culmination of theories by twentieth-century scientists such as Edwin Hubble, Albert Einstein, Aleksander Friedmann, George Ganau, and termed by Fred Hoyle in 1950. It was mind-blowing to see that although the Big Bang was conceptualised as recently as the twentieth century, it was mentioned in the Quran in AD 600.

Dr Zakir Naik, a physician and international orator on comparative religions stated, "How could a book, which first appeared in the deserts of Arabia 1400 years ago, contain this profound scientific truth?"

The Big Bang theory is an attempt to describe the creation and evolution of the universe. Science tells us it is pointless to go back beyond the Big Bang and meaningless to ask what came before, because there is no before; nothing existed before. Time itself, is supposed to have come into existence with the Big Bang.

"Nothing" has a very special meaning in this context. It literally means nothing, the complete absence of everything, so nothing must be an infinite void. This empty space has no boundaries or dimensions, as a dimension would be a boundary. Nothing then, when described as an infinite void, excludes all possibility of anything else existing anywhere. Therefore, nothing existed before, and now, because we exist and our universe exists, nothing can ever exist in the future, either.

It's amazing how Stephen Hawking also relates to the Big Bang as having the no boundary concept before its occurrence.
"The universe has not existed forever. Rather, the universe, and time itself, had a beginning, which was the Big Bang, about 15 billion years ago. The way the universe began would have been determined by the laws of physics, if the universe satisfied the no boundary condition. This says that in the imaginary time direction, space-time is finite in extent, but doesn't have any boundary or edge. The predictions of the no boundary proposal seem to agree with observation. The no boundary hypothesis also predicts that the universe will eventually collapse again".

I could go on debating the theory of the Big Bang, but it's a huge topic on its own. However, the striking similarity between the Quranic verses and the Big Bang theory is inescapable. The splitting of the heavens and the earth refers to the occurrence of the Big Bang. The enormous explosion describes the very beginning of time itself.

As an artist who perceives everything in a creative dimension, I had visions of my interpretation of these profound passages from the Quran. I felt inspired and compelled by this information, this knowledge, this revelation which I now possessed. I couldn't wait to stand in front of my canvas to try and make sense of it all. I was so enthralled by visions of what these smokey, gaseous matters could be and how I could express this in a non-representational form. What is meant by the splitting of the heavens and earth? And what does this mean to me as an artist? I wanted to create work that expressed the excitement within me which I wanted to share through my art.

I created paintings such as the Big Bang (oil on canvas) and the Splitting of the Heavens and the Earth (oil on canvas) to illustrate faith and science coming together on the notion of the beginning of creation.

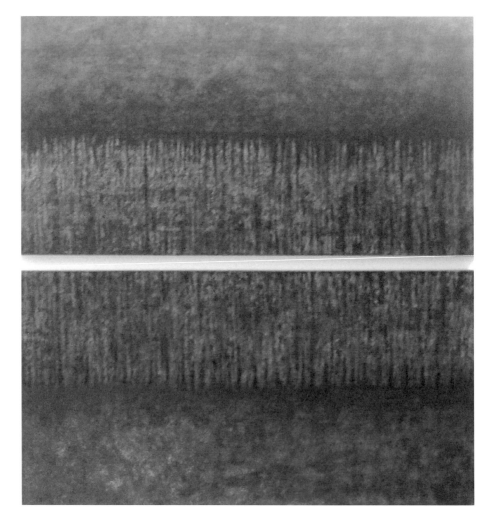

Splitting of the Heavens and the Earth, oil on canvas 2007, by Aisha Cahn.

CHAPTER 2
THE EXISTENCE OF GOD

As God is abstract, people throughout time have found it difficult to put their trust and belief into something that is unseen, unknown, and cannot be felt or heard. So they turned to what they believed was sublime – the sun, the moon, stars, and water. All are aesthetically extraordinary aspects of nature, which they began to refer to as God and to worship them. They could not comprehend that all of creation came from a physically non-existent being.

God is universal, and I feel this is the basic commonality amongst all humankind (with the exception of a very few) which should unite us in a homogenous way. Instead, through this commonality, there seems to be the widest division in the name of religion that has torn apart humankind and created the worse sort of animosity and hatred amongst themselves. By observing God's different names and attributes that constitute every aspect of nature and life, I attempted to create a paradox in my work through the expression of unity, instead of division, amongst humankind.

My series on the Creation of the Universe required me to research every aspect of creation through both science and religion. Learning about scientific discoveries from the beginning of time, exploring every aspect of God's creation, and reading verses from the sacred scriptures made it possible for me to comprehend the existence of God. The Quran, in particular, has been fundamental in this investigation. Texts expound in great detail the expansion of the universe, the formation of stars and galaxies, and the alternation of night and day in perfect harmony. God's creation of humans from a drop of sperm and a clot of blood developed into human life behind three veils of darkness in the mother's womb. He enlightened this human life with His own spirit; the soul and life of our existence.

Given that scientists have proved God's existence through several aspects of His creation by way of theories and experiments, we need not rely simply on faith and belief any longer. Although it is sad to see people need to have tangible proof to accept God's existence and creation, it was declared in the Holy Scriptures centuries ago that there is an abundance of proof all around us, that we have taken completely for granted.

During his life, Isaac Newton (1642–1727) began to describe the physical universe with God as an essential part of its system. The notion of gravitational force, which Newton introduced, offended many scientists and was incompatible with the Protestant view of the absolute sovereignty of God. Newton wrote, "Gravity may put ye planets into motion but without ye divine power it could never put them into such a circulating motion as they have about ye Sun, and therefore, for this as well as other reasons, I am compelled to ascribe ye frame of this System to an intelligent Agent."

Newton concluded that this agent had to be extremely powerful to manage and control such an intricate system. He believed the influence had to be that of the divine God. To Newton, contemplation of the world led to the knowledge of God. He described how God constitutes time and space, and explained that matter was created by God on the day of creation of a celestial matter in the form of gaseous clouds, causing a dark smoky atmosphere – the Big Bang.

A Neoplatonist philosopher, Solomon ibn Gabirol (1022–1070) also argued, "God had created the world at a particular moment; the world had certainly not come into being by accident: that would be as ridiculous an idea as imagining that a perfectly written paragraph came into being when ink was spilled on a page. The order and purpose-ness of the world shows that there must be a Creator, as the scriptures revealed."

On the other hand, Rene Descartes (1596–1650), a mathematician and zealous Catholic, insisted that intellect alone and the ability of the mind were all humans needed to discover God. Instead of using the world to prove the existence of God, Descartes used the idea of God to give him faith in the reality of the world. He deduced facts about the nature of God the same way he conducted mathematical demonstrations.

The Iranian philosopher Abu Hamid Al-Ghazzali (1058–1111) concluded, "If we claimed to understand God, that would mean that He is finite and imperfect. The most exact statement we could make about God is that He is incomprehensible, and utterly transcending. He continues to explain that it was not possible to prove God's existence logically, but neither was it possible to disprove it."

The search for a higher power has been chaotic and desolate to the universe, with humans causing unrest in the attempt to prove God's existence and being left frustrated, unhappy, and despairing when neither proof of God's existence nor His non-existence has been possible. Since such proof is impossible, faith that comes from within the heart is the only reliable factor.

God is the One and Only Supreme Spirit, Who alone exists of Himself and is Infinite in all perfections. He is A Transcendental Being at a level beyond comprehension. If there were more than one God, this would lead to confusion, disorder, chaos, and destruction in the operation of the universe, which is in perfect harmony.

Ever since the dawn of human life, humankind has always tried to understand nature and its own place in the scheme of creation and the purpose of life itself. In this search for truth, spanning many centuries and diverse civilisations, religion has shaped human life and determined the course of history.

The God of the Jews, Christians, and Muslims is a God who, in a sense, speaks. His world is crucial in all three faiths and has determined the creation of our culture. He fashioned the world in six days, as mentioned in the book of Genesis, the Old Testament of the Bible, and in The Quran (7:54).

How could a material world have its origin in a wholly spiritual God? Karen Armstrong, author of *The History of God*, explains;
Here we had reached the limits of reason and must simply accept that the world is not eternal, but had a beginning in time. This was the only possible explanation that agreed with all scriptures and commo n sense. Once we have accepted this, we can deduce other facts about God: the created order is intelligently planned; it has life and energy. Therefore God, who created it, must also have Wisdom, Life and Power. These attributes are mere aspects of God, but because our human language cannot adequately express thc reality of God or the mind cannot comprehend the Creation of the Universe, that we have to analyse Him in this way and seem to destroy His absolute simplicity. If we want to be as exact about God as possible, we can only properly say He exists.

In an article by A M Omar, former editor of Encyclopedia of Islam; Allah is the mighty name of thc Self-Existing and Self-Sufficient Being, Who comprises all perfect attributes and is free from every weakness and defect. He alone is worthy of worship and is without partner or peer. He is the source of all love and grace and beyond all comparison. So transcendent is He, and so far above all material conception, that a likeness of Him cannot be conceived. Vision comprehends Him not, and He comprehends all vision. He cannot be fully comprehended or grasped by the human mind. We do not speak of "It" when we mention Allah; we speak of Him. This shows that Allah is better understood as being personal rather than impersonal. He has a will (Quran 3:26) and a purpose

(Quran 51:56). He is a Spiritual Being without a physical body (Quran 24:35) and is not bound by the limitations of time and space which besets physical bodies. The attributes of Allah are the most valuable dues we possess to know Him.

This is the most comprehensive and intelligent explanation of the perception of God that I have come across. Apart from this very simplified and plausible explanation of the Almighty God, there is so much proof around us that requires no explanation but a mere acceptance of there being an incredible intellectual, luminous force of energy to have created the universe and the world we live in. My belief in the existence of God has also been reaffirmed by observing how people have tried to prove His existence since the beginning of time, and how irrespective of the centuries of research, investigations, and experiments, no one has been able to prove His non-existence to date.

One's belief in God requires no condition; a rejection of God does. It is better to return to the classic explanation that God is greater than human beings, and His thoughts and ways are incomprehensible. People have the choice of trusting this indescribable God and affirming a meaning, even amid meaninglessness.

God is so sublime. He is something that cannot be comprehended or measured in any shape or form by our limited intelligence. It's difficult to come to terms with the notion of The God whom I am in such awe of. And to think that so many people are unsure of the existence of this unknown phenomenon. Yet, I feel He is so close to me, so close to my heart. I feel I have an unconditional love for this incredible, amazing, irrational, sublime force of luminous energy.

There is so much evidence around us that denotes the existence of God. One doesn't have to look far to see how beautifully planned and organised the world is and how the operations of the planets are so well coordinated without any contributions from us. Humans have never had to worry about the alternation of the sun and the moon, the growth of vegetation, the spirit of life in living beings, or the creation of life from water. Over time, humankind has continually complicated matters by trying to prove something the limited mind does not have the ability to comprehend.

In his book *Chromophobia*, author David Bachelor attempts to illustrate how one is drawn towards complexities and convolutions. Neutrality and beauty can be viewed as a kind of perversity in the same way innocence can be seen as evil. He writes how some people perceive colour as a symbol of disorder and anti-liberty; as a drug that can intoxicate; and as a corrupt, dangerous, and disruptive creation.

I suppose this is just another example of how people can misrepresent and distort. Evil can be seen as good, and good as evil. Not even colour is beyond negative criticism. It is an absurd argument. It is difficult to understand how something so pure, so vibrant, and so demure and calming can be compared to something so corrupt or destructive. People sometimes miss the point that God has shown us colour through the rainbow, and these colours can be expressed through the beauty of nature. The colours of nature and the spectrum of light create such vibrancy and demure emotions within oneself that one should just enjoy the aesthetic and psychological effect it exudes and be creative with it. As an artist and a painter, I am still exploring ways to express the Infinite and Sublime form of God through the finite physicality and beauty of the infinite use of colour.

My understanding of this life is that we are the children of Adam and Eve. Truly understanding the underlying message of the three Abrahamic religions has lead me to the clear understanding of Islam as the complete religion and the amalgamation of Judaism and Christianity.

In light of what God has bestowed on us, our meagre thanks do not compare. He has given us the gifts of hearing, sight, smell, touch, and taste to fill our lives with sensations and experiences. He has given us intelligence to progress and succeed. He has given us freedom of choice and vast opportunities, so we can differentiate between good and bad and make the right or wrong decisions through life.

Every slight movement in the world – the rise of the sun, the rotation of the earth upon its axis, the rush of water, and the stirring of the wind – is God's work, all of which we take totally for granted every day. How many of us wake up every morning and wonder, *What would happen if the sun didn't rise today?* Probably most of the world's population. But because He has ordained the sun to rise like clockwork at various times, according to its time zone in the various parts of the world, we completely take His mercies and favours upon us for granted.

In the series titled *Elements of Nature,* I created a polyptych of six canvases titled "The Circle of Nature. The thought process behind this title is that the world needs the four elements to function in cycle. If any of these elements didn't function, the world could not survive.

My quest for the purpose of existence enabled me to realise that life is really simpler than we make it out to be. I cannot thank God enough for making me a part of His beautiful creation. I thank Him daily through my prayers and remembrance of Him. I find myself becoming closer to God every single day, something that has been increasing progressively throughout the past ten years of my life, when this journey began.

I have formed such a loving bond with the Almighty God that I turn to Him whenever I need to. I talk to Him about my children, my family, my life and any problems I may face. I turn to Him for new forms of inspiration for my work, when I have reached a crossroad in my studio, and my mind is void of ideas. I ask Him to help humankind stay united and for peace and harmony throughout the world. Most of all, I ask Him for guidance, patience, and tolerance in everything I say and do. We can spend our entire lives attempting to prove or disprove the existence of God. However, till today, this has been an impossible feat.

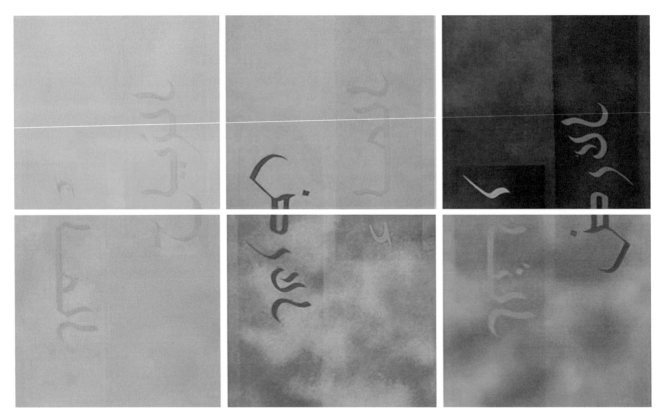

Circle of Nature, polyptych, mixed media, and oil on canvas, 2011, by Aisha Cahn.

CHAPTER 3
ABOUT MY WORK

An approach to dealing with the experience of God's presence through art has been evident throughout history. The fields of religion and art have been intertwined since the beginning of time to present day. Religion has served as a motive and starting point for the creation of artworks throughout time. Artists have used their medium to glorify, protest, enquire, idealise, and tell their stories of religion.

While I was studying Arabic as a language with Nora, I fell in love with the beautiful Arabic letters. There were so many styles of this elegant script, each one more beautiful than the next. I wanted to learn more about the Arabic script and how it came together to deliver such profound messages fourteen hundred years ago. I searched for a calligraphy master and was lucky enough to meet a Palestinian Arabic calligraphy master, Mr Abu Mustafa, who came to my house once a month. He taught me the differences between the various Arabic calligraphic scripts and educated me about their historic and chronological formations.

I now began learning about each individual Arabic letter and how they are formed and linked to compile words and sentences. I was more drawn to the Kufic script from the very beginning. It is the oldest form of Arabic script, and many of the early Qurans were written in this script. Kufic developed around the end of the seventh century in Kufa, Iraq, from which it takes its name. It has very angular and linear letters that remind me of the Art Deco era, which I have always had an affinity for; my home in London is a listed Art Deco building.

Mr Mustafa talked me through each of the twenty-eight letters of the Arabic alphabet. He wrote them on paper, and I practiced rewriting them with precision for the entire month, before my next session with him. He used special wooden pens (the reed pen) crafted specifically for Arabic calligraphy. He gifted me a few which I then used with different colours of Indian ink to do my homework. When we reconvened every month, Mr Mustafa corrected all the imperfections in my lettering as he was very particular about the characters. I soon progressed to forming words and placing them within sentences. I thoroughly enjoyed these sessions with him. We often had lengthy discussions about Islam. I continued studying with him for a year, until we both felt I was confident enough with my Kufic script to set out on my own.

I wanted to stylise the Kufic script in a way it would become recognised by everyone that this was an Aisha Cahn style of Arabic calligraphy. I suppose because of my background as a fashion designer, where I had my own style of illustrating, I wanted to implement my style into this beautiful script. I decided I wanted to be more creative with this new talent/skill of mine. I felt that I had achieved my own style by now and wanted to apply it to a form of Fine Art. I didn't really know much about the different media related to it, although I did Art O 'Level and Art A Level in Textile Design. My first degree was in Fashion Design at the London College of Fashion, but my creative skills there, were used in creating designs for womenswear and fashion illustrating, far removed from the world of Fine Art.

I knew I had to manifest these visions of the creation of the universe and its Creator, and the application of Arabic calligraphy into some form of creative medium, but I felt restricted in skill and tools. I therefore embarked on three intensive short courses of watercolour, oil painting, and mixed media at Central St Martin's (CSM) College of Art and Design. Whilst attending these short courses, my subject matter remained constant. I thoroughly enjoyed this new adventure of discovery of not just my subject but my medium and my ever-exploring mind.

I preferred the oil painting and the mixed-media courses over the watercolour course. I found watercolour far more difficult than the other two courses. The paint dried very quickly as it was water based, and because of this, you could see the brush marks and dry patches on the painted surfaces. The technique really needed to have finesse to it, and I guess I just didn't have the patience for it.

What I loved about oil painting was that you could just splatter the paint on or pile the paint on with a spatula, creating layers upon layers. You could be delicate with the paint or vigorous. I also liked the different textures you could create with oil paint by applying various media to it. I liked the fact that oil paint and mixed media create some very interesting surfaces and compositions. With oil painting and mixed media, I could paint on large canvasses and just let myself go and be free-spirited. I found myself reflecting on how the abstract expressionist artists created their large canvasses.

Abstract Expressionism was about; painting large, splattering, drip painting, solid backgrounds, gestural painting, action painting, deep hues, spiritual and mystical subjects, emotional spontaneity, the unconscious mind, and so on. Although many of the abstract expressionists' works give the impression of spontaneity, most of these paintings involved careful planning, especially since their large canvasses demanded it.

After finishing my short courses at CSM, I wanted to experiment and put what I studied into practice. So I enrolled in various Professional Development courses at Kensington & Chelsea College (KCC) to help me explore the entire field of Fine Art. My aim was to develop as an artist professionally, and I stayed at KCC for three years, training for a career in Fine Art. This whole thing really started as a hobby, but as I so enjoyed exploring this new creative talent of mine, I decided to apply to do an MA Degree in Fine Art, despite at such a late stage in my life. I am an all-or-nothing person, and if I put my mind to doing something, I put my heart and soul into it completely and approach it with utmost dedication and passion. I will follow the path in a professional manner and obtain professional help and guidance – as with the Arabic teacher, the calligraphy master, and my short courses.

After deciding that I wanted to be a practicing artist, I applied to Central St Martin's College of Art and Design to further hone my skills. I was very fortunate to receive a place in the Institution's part-time MA Degree course in Fine Art. I was extremely glad the course spanned over two years, so I could take the time to focus on my processes and techniques to develop my art practice. This was really the start of my Fine Art career. I absorbed the content and subject matter of the study programme, which I knew would form the essence and framework of my later work. Having embarked on a second career so late in life, I never wasted any opportunity to learn and began to research and document my thoughts and source of inspirations for the MA programme.

This programme was based on my spiritual journey through life, which I had recently embarked on. It was manifested through a series of canvasses, each being a window looking into various aspects of God's creation, fusing abstract and visual representation and Arabic calligraphic text. I experimented with creating unusual textural surfaces inspired by many abstract expressionist artists. I was particularly drawn to Jackson Pollock's drip painting titled *Summertime: Number 9,* which forms part of the permanent collection at Tate Modern. In many of his drip paintings, and this one in particular, Pollock creates black, sticklike rhythmic silhouettes amongst an array of layers of carefully arranged drips of paint. These silhouettes reminded me very much of Arabic calligraphic forms.

Allahu Akbar 2, mixed media on paper, 2006, by Aisha Cahn.

As I researched Pollock's work, it seemed particularly relevant to examine the works of other American Abstract Expressionist artists of the 1940s and 1950s, especially Mark Rothko and Barnett Newman, whose works are very spiritual and contemplative, which informs my work. Abstract expressionist art was associated with the way in which these artists worked. Abstract art clearly implied expression of ideas concerning the spiritual, the unconscious, and the mind.

I experienced this form of contemplation which was very surreal when I sat in the Red Room at Tate Modern. The room, which was quite dark and dimly lit, had seven huge paintings by Mark Rothko. They created an aura of something quite spectacular and yet tranquil. The sheer size of these paintings and the relationship between the scale of Rothko's paintings and the viewer is overwhelming. Whilst observing these paintings of various shapes, forms, and tones of reds, maroons, browns, and blacks, my mind and imagination were immersed in these vast dimensions of space and colour. I felt numb because for that moment, I was thinking of nothing. This 'nothing' was a form of transcendence as for that time, I felt I was not part of this material world. I found myself lost in this space of being un-found. I found myself looking with the heart as well as the curious eye. I realised there was far more to these paintings than what the eye sees, if we are to understand even a small part of what its creator intended. Emptying the mind of preconceptions or distractions clears space that can draw us in.

Andrej Tisma, a Yugoslavian artist, art critic, curator, and activist, stated in an article on Art and Religion in 1994, "It is time to bring back spirituality, which is the link to the meaning of existence, it is time for art and religion to meet again. In art, religion has its place as much as spiritual art does."

It is an encouraging coincidence to read such a statement by Tisma as this is exactly what I am endeavouring to do in my art practice. I am trying to put back the significance of religion and God in its original and true sense, since much of the origin and history of art is grounded in religious themes and expression, and not in a way which dismisses or trivializes the religious, as many contemporary artists have done during the past few decades.

My feeling is that humankind has forgotten how to be curious about religion or the genesis of things. I am therefore trying to create a renaissance, a kind of religious/sacred art in a contemporary form.

It is ironic that with my Eastern and Islamic heritage, I am influenced by and drawn to Western artists. My work is regarded as a hybrid, bridging the two cultures of East and West, just as the seen invites the less-understood unseen to be experienced by the viewer. For my own work, and by using Arabic calligraphy in my paintings, the hidden purpose becomes clear when the viewer develops a state of contemplation while trying to make sense of this beautiful, stylized, and angular form of text. Although it may be an alien concept to Western eyes, this language creates a visual dialogue within the overall composition of my paintings.

In some of my work, the paint has extended beyond the boundary of the canvas and onto the wall space. By doing this, I am expressing that there are no boundaries or limitations to one's imagination. However, the boundaries of the canvas do exist, just as we exist. But although we are governed by boundaries and limitations, which we must abide by, we are all capable of transgressing. Therefore, we also have no boundaries because we have the freedom of choice to do anything we want, be it right or wrong. I am by no means trying to express infinity, because the world we live in has boundaries, dimensions, and limitations. But it is a metaphor of the mind.

Earth, oil on canvas and extended onto the wall, 2008 by Aisha Cahn.

Art is a form of expression through various media, including sculpture, painting, installation, music, film, and theatre. It is the universal manifestation of an artist's thoughts, through which he or she shares ideas, experiences, memories, and journeys with the rest of the world in a creative and innovative form.

This expression also reflects the artists' cultures and social environments, which differ from country to country and across the hemispheres. Regardless of the applied media, art is largely appreciated through its aesthetics; these are what viewers interpret in their own ways and appreciate regardless of culture and demographic differences. Because of the way art is appreciated globally, it has been a real turning point in my life to use this medium to express my journey through life.

I think it was the MA programme in Fine Art which confirmed I would express my beliefs about the existence of God and my newfound spiritual inner self of contentment through my artwork.

I hired a studio when I began the MA programme; I felt I would work much better in my own space. Although I had converted our at-home gym into a studio, it was impossible to get any work done there. The phone would constantly be ringing, my housekeeper would periodically approach me about various issues concerning the house, and there were always several forms of distraction from my two daughters. My two daughters, Jemma-Lia and Hanah, were enrolled in their respective universities at the time but only had approximately ten hours of lectures per week, which meant they were at home rather frequently and proved to be my biggest distractions.

My first studio was a tiny little space – approximately one hundred square feet – at Canalot Studios in London. I will always remember my first day of being there. Once I moved all my things into the studio – easels, tables, canvasses, paints, pencils, sketchbooks, etc. – I closed the door behind me and simply leaned against it, looking around. The walls were white and blank. A large window overlooked the canal, exhibiting the most beautiful view. I thought, *This is my space, and nobody can disturb me here.* I was all by myself, surrounded by these white walls and my canvasses. I could now focus and concentrate fully on creating wonderful works of art to adorn these huge white walls.

I would not listen to any music in my studio because I felt the nature of my subject matter required me to be holistically inspired, enabling my mind, body, and soul to partake collectively in producing each piece of work. I began to source my inspiration from audio recitations of the Quran. I was always very particular about the type of audio recordings I listened to because an Imam with a strong and graceful voice can penetrate the soul with his narration. Listening to the beautiful words of God, enabled me to immerse myself in my work. During this time, I also began to listen to narrations on other topics, such as the "Purification of the Soul", by Haroon Yahya; Introduction to Sufism; The Life of the Prophet Mohammed (PBUH), and The Lives and Stories of The Prophets. These narratives further helped me to acquire inspiration for my work and more importantly, made me reflect on the simplicity of life. I implemented several of these ideas in a series of paintings for one of my major exhibitions, *titled Creation*, later in 2011.

I stayed at Canalot Studios until April 2007, after which I moved to a slightly larger space at the Saga Centre on Kensal Road. I was approaching my final year of the MA degree course, and I wanted to produce larger pieces of work at that stage, while still concentrating on being as innovative, creative, and explorative as I could with my work.

In 2007, I went on the pilgrimage journey to Makkah, Saudi Arabia, and performed the rituals of the Hajj, which every Muslim aspires to perform at least once in his or her lifetime. The circumambulation of the Ka'abah (the house of God), the slaughtering of lambs, and stoning of the devil are some of the rituals that were set during the time of the Prophet Abraham and are still practiced today. These symbolic acts have been known to infiltrate the hearts and minds of people during the pilgrimage, along with being conscious of the strong presence of Allah in the Holy Land.

Muslims from all over the world – regardless of race, nationality, or status – flock to the Haram, the Sacred Mosque, for the sole purpose of worshipping Allah. Allah, whom I also refer to as the "Sublime", is abstract. He cannot be seen, touched, or heard. Yet through this absence, I felt His presence so evidently within myself and in the Holy Land. This form of abstraction was so vast, so very powerful, and so sublime that I felt spiritually moved and completely overwhelmed.

It was the most incredibly spiritual experience I could have ever imagined to encounter during my lifetime. It was a journey that brought me forth from darkness into light; darkness referring to this materialistic world full of temptation and greed, and light being the form of enlightenment that enters and dispels this shadow.

The darkness is incapable of comprehending such light, the same way the human's finite mind is unable to understand or explain what is infinite. When spiritual light pierces the inner self, the heart, it generates awareness within us. We then can be conscious of our subconscious behaviours. As I became more conscious of my inner self, it made me aware of the spiritual aspect of my faith. This spiritual aspect of Islam is known as Sufism.

Extracts from *Turning Towards the Heart,* Awakening to the Sufi Way, by Shaykh al Tariqat Hazrat Azad Rasool.
Sufism, Tasawwuf as it is known in the Muslim world, is Islamic mysticism. It adheres to all the fundamentals of the religion and focusses on the ultimate truth. The meaning of Sufism is the selfless experiencing and actualisation of the truth. The practice of Sufism is the intention to go towards the truth by means of love and devotion to God. This is called the tariqat, the spiritual path or way towards God. The Sufi is a lover of truth, who by means of love and devotion from the heart moves towards the Truth, towards the perfection which we all are truly seeking. The Quran

recognises the validity of 120,000 prophets who have come to awaken us from our selfish egoism and reminds us of our spiritual nature of selflessness.

"Mystical experience activates the self, the I, which brings about a certain degree of consciousness and insight. This degree of consciousness makes one aware of God acting in and through creation. Many people attain this level of awareness at some point in their lives, and I guess mine was this beautiful experience of my pilgrimage to Makkah.
This led me to follow a Sufi Order, a path which focusses on achieving unity between the outer and inner beings, as this will otherwise interfere with turning towards the Divine, the purification of the soul and by awakening the heart through meditation and *dhikr* (remembrance of God)".

I could really go on talking about Sufism forever, but this is just a brief insight into the spiritual aspect of Islam. Belonging to a Sufi Order, has enabled me to put things in perspective and obtain a form of realisation as to what really matters in life. Life isn't about me, me, me; it's about you, my fellow human being. It is about detaching oneself from this materialistic world and focussing on purifying one's soul through remembering God and finding a way to connect with Him and to show love for Him.

On my return to London from Makkah, I explored the concept of abstraction in greater depth, both in daily spiritual practices and through my art practice. Until that moment, all my paintings either had the name of Allah in them or a verse from the Quran expressing His existence. It was a form of dhikr. However, after returning from Makkah, I realised that I could continue to create a presence of God through my paintings in a form of abstract art.

By experimenting and playing with colour blocks and layers of colour to represent certain aspects of the creation of the universe and bringing forth the presence of God through creating luminosity to represent the light of God within the paintings, I felt it was not always necessary to use Arabic text in my work.

The paintings titled *Day* and *Night* (mixed media & and oil on canvas) each have verses from the Quran to explain the beauty of God's creations. *Day* reads, "Allah made the sun to be a shining glory and the moon to be a light of beauty." *Night* reads, "Allah makes the night overlap the day and day overlap the night." They convey the message that not only is nature an exquisite creation, it functions in perfect and complete harmony, with every single movement vital and significant.

I created similar paintings depicting Daylight and Moonlight, but this time created the luminosity of the light of God within these very abstract paintings, as a result of the spiritual experience from my pilgrimage to Makkah.

Jean Francis Lyotard explains in his book *Sublime and the Avant Garde*, "To make visible something, which can be conceived; and which can neither be seen nor made visible; and how to make visible that there is something, which cannot be seen."

Immanuel Kant shows the way through formlessness, "the absence of, as a possible index to the unpresentable."

Lyotard helped me understand the challenge I had faced earlier when attempting to express an unknown phenomenon, such as God, through the practice of Fine Art, as all media is a form of physical matter. This challenge of the unknown world emerges into the realm of spirituality, where the imagination runs freely into the depths of formlessness. For me, Kant has also explained this so well that he helped me understand the challenge in trying to present the unrepresentable.

The empty abstraction of time and space, which the imagination experiences through the search for presentation of the sublime, is void of figuration and representation. My reference to the Sublime is God, and I have not associated it with anything else. However, in aesthetics, the sublime refers to the quality of greatness or vast imagination, whether physical, moral, intellectual, metaphysical, or artistic.

According to Lyotard, "the sublime is not strictly speaking, something that is proven or demonstrated, but a marvel, which seizes one, strikes one and makes one feel in awe."

Kant adds, "the sublime is a force that is greater than the human, which holds the human beings in a state of awe. The sublime cannot be comprehended by individuals, who can at best come to recognise the incomprehensibility of the magnitude and power, and their inferiority before it."

The work for my final MA Degree exhibition in 2008 was about God's creation of the universe, a theme for which the sky was the limit. Within this vast expanse of space, I could explore art and ideas in anyway I desired. God gave me the freedom to express my thoughts, observations, and understanding of the purpose of life.

During my MA Degree Show at Central St Martin's, my father was terribly unwell. He was diagnosed with Emphysema at the time and attached to an oxygen cylinder. He was out of breath as soon as he arrived at my exhibition space in the college and had to take a seat immediately on arrival. While sitting down and trying to get his breath back, he spent his time silently observing all my paintings on show. One painting in particular caught his eye. Once he got his breath back, he said, "Take me to that painting, darling," pointing to the large 7'x 7' canvas titled *Allah The Omnipresent*. After I helped him get closer to the painting, he stood in front of it and just gazed at it for some time, his eyes full of emotion; he appeared to be in a state of deep contemplation. He then quietly said, "This painting was drawing me in and calling me to it as I was sitting down. I absolutely love it."

This was a large painting in monochromatic tonalities of yellows, creams, and stony colours. Within these colours, the name of Allah illuminates through, creating the most beautiful form of luminosity.

The viewers were keen to learn about my inspirations and to understand the extent of my research and thought process. They seemed to relate to the fusion of science and faith, and my work was now regarded as a hybrid, bridging the two cultures of East and West

I created *Mountains* to demonstrate how the Quran states that mountains were deeply rooted in the foundation of the earth's surface to stabilise the crust of the earth and prevent it from shaking. "And we have set on the earth mountains standing firm, lest it should shake with them" (Quran 21:31). "And the mountains hath He firmly fixed" (Quran 79:32).

Some people may think the nature of my work is controversial as I try to convey the essence of faith and the notion of God in a realistic and respectful manner. Most art creates some form of controversy, irrespective of its subject matter. It's important to create art that evokes this reaction, which I feel is necessary. There needs to be some form of an emotional reaction, a dialogue almost, between the viewer and the painting, be it good or bad.

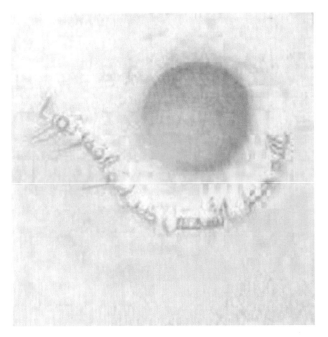

Day, mixed media on canvas,
2007 by Aisha Cahn.

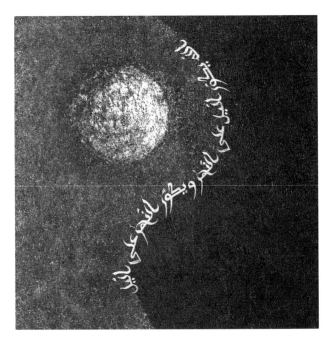

Night, mixed media on canvas,
2007 by Aisha Cahn.

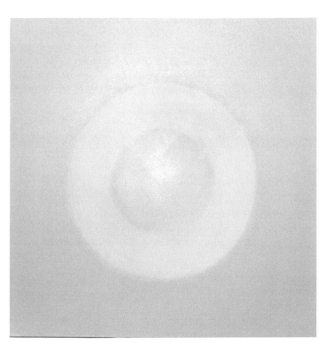

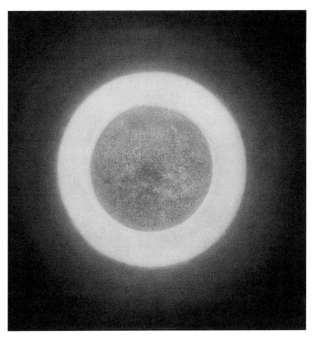

Daylight, oil on canvas, 2009 by Aisha Cahn.

Moonlight, oil on canvas, 2009 by Aisha Cahn

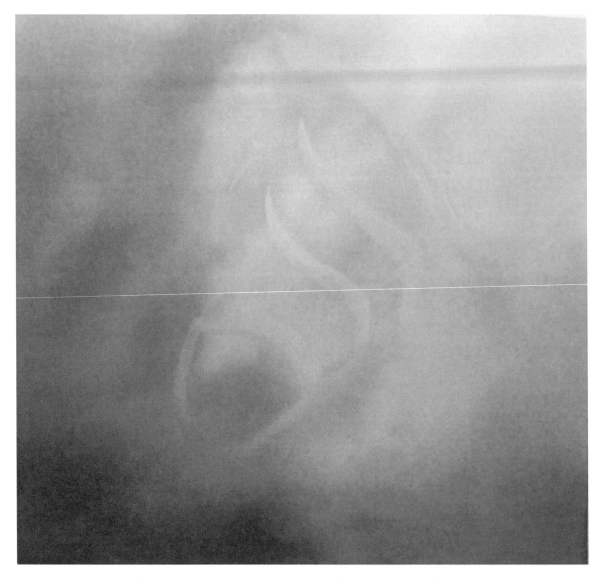

The Omnipresent, oil on canvas, 2008, by Aisha Cahn.

CHAPTER 4
THE DISCIPLINES OF FAITH, SCIENCE, AND ART

Art and religion have gone hand in hand for thousands of years, and the two fields have permeated each other since the beginning of time. Religion has served as a motive and starting point for the creation of art. Art commissioned by religion has been one of the strongest manifesting aspects of the human spirit.

Art glorifies, protests, idealises, and depicts religion. During periods of history, art existed for the sake of religion. Religion dominated art, commissioning it and using it for propaganda. During the Italian Renaissance, artists such as Leonardo da Vinci and Michelangelo were commissioned by the church to produce works of art depicting the Madonna and Christ as a child and the classic painting of *The Hand of God,* by Michelangelo. Christianity was going through its own Reformation during the fifteenth and sixteenth centuries, and people were beginning to lose faith in religion and the church.

Renaissance art can be considered religious art as we recognise the images and know the stories. Ceilings and walls were painted to give the illusion of infinity. Narratives of gospel stories were drawn to create a world where saints, disciples, Jesus, and Mary were real, earthly beings filled with life. During the eighth and ninth centuries, several images and icons were destroyed with the blessing of the Pope because of the second commandment of the Old Testament, which forbids the making of graven images.

However, during the Reformation, the Roman Catholic Church became a victim of iconoclasm and lost many religious images of great artistic value. However, religion, like art, often consists of a dialogue with the past to find a vantage point from which to assess the present.

Exodus 20:4 reads, "Do not make for yourselves images of anything in the heaven or on earth or in the water under the earth." It's amazing to see such a vast collection of iconic figurative artworks in many museums and art galleries despite this verse.

The Islamic faith also forbids the representation of living creatures because of the danger of idolatry. This is why there are rich, abstract designs in mosques rather than pictures or drawings of Prophets. Islamic art focusses on the spiritual representation of objects and beings, not their physical qualities. Geometric patterns are used to represent nature and objects through their spiritual qualities of infinite occurrence. This is thought to reflect the language of the universe, where the believer reflects on life and the greatness of creation. Both the artist and the viewer are said to feel closer to Allah through the beauty and symbolism of this form of art. Beauty has always been and will always be a quality of the Divine.

Every work of art must have a creator and the Creator of the Universe is Allah (God).

There have been many manifestations of God represented through forms of figurative art, especially in the Hindu faith. The Hindus believe the Super Being must be anthropomorphic. This anthropomorphic trinity comprises of Vishnu, Shiva, and Brahma. Each is a manifestation of the Super Being, performing different functions. Brahma is the creator, Vishnu the preserver, and Shiva the destroyer.

The sixteenth century was a crucial period for the Christian West. It saw the Italian Renaissance, which quickly spread to Northern Europe; the discovery of the New World; and the scientific revolution. Despite their success, people were more concerned about their faith than ever before, splitting Europe into two warring camps, Catholic and Protestant. The Reformers were nearly all associated with some form of mysticism. The experience of God was not regarded as a clog but as a form of transformation that would hasten the transition to modernity. Those who believe in the evolution theory do not believe in the concept of God.

David Rosevar, in the introduction to his book *Creation Science* (1991), calls the evolution theory, "the scientific arm of atheistic humanism." Atheism is "non-belief in, or denial of a god or gods," while Humanism is, "a 20th-century philosophy which rejects religious belief, claiming that people are capable of achieving happiness and behaving morally without any divine guidance."[1]

Although atheists deny the existence of God, they are forever soul-searching because they cannot prove His non-existence, and there is no morality without religion.

---

[1] David Rosevar, *Creation Science,* 9.

Atheism has always been a rejection of a current conception of the divine. Jews and Muslims were called atheists because they denied the pagan notion of the divine.

A common feature of all major religions is the belief in a universal God or Supreme Divine Authority that is Omnipotent and Omniscient. However, Marxism, Freudianism, and other non-religious beliefs tried to attack the roots of organised religions and disbelieved in the existence of God.

The nineteenth century saw the rise of atheism in the West. People of the Christian faith were vulnerable to the scientific discoveries, which revealed the vast perspectives of Charles Darwin's *The Origin of Species.* Theories, over time, become popular, survive for a time, and are then overturned by subsequent generations. This account of the evolutionary hypothesis was in total contradiction to the Bible, Torah, and the Quran. Simply because we cannot prove God's existence in a way which can satisfy scientific standards does not mean He doesn't exist.

The exhibition *Sacred* at the British Library in June 2006 displayed an interesting selection of sacred scriptures. The oldest was the Chester Beatty manuscript, the earliest surviving manuscript dated about AD 250.

Walder Januszczak of the *Daily Mail* wrote,

Sacred sets out to prove that, at heart, Christianity, Judaism and Islam are remarkably similar and share numerous habits, heroes and histories. The three religions emerged in the same region in similar social circumstances. All three worship a single God, called Allah in one faith, Jehovah and Hesham in the other two, but transparently the same deity. All three have at their centre a book – The Bible, The Quran and The Torah, whose function is to provide its followers with a fixed and incorruptible supply of the word. That's what this show is about, the power of the word. If there is one thing these religions really do share, it is the reliance on the efficacy of their books. The British Library has brought together a remarkable assortment of precious writings to make the point that, while the three religions are certainly not interchangeable, they are, in the main, excellently congruent.

Most European artworks produced in the past thousand years have had obvious religious content, but the artists themselves may not have necessarily been religiously inspired or spiritually moved. One of the most recognisable images of Western culture is Michelangelo's portrayal of God's hand reaching out to Adam's. The image of two fingers almost touching in the cracked fresco in the Sistine Chapel has dominated Western imaginations for almost five hundred years.

An extract from Lindsay Farrell, *The Hand of God in the Art of Michelangelo;*
"The way we see and recall images affects us at a fundamental level of our consciousness. The visual language used in the representation of those two hands has permeated more thoroughly than any verbal language our collective imaginations and thinking about the nature of God humankind".[2]

This is a classic interpretation of God being in an anthropomorphic form. God is not human-like. He hears but not with ears like our ears; He sees but not with eyes like our eyes. We read that His hands are stretched; this means that He is full of bounties. Thus, the hands of God spoken in the Quran 5:64 express His unlimited power, favour, and protection. God's throne does not signify any place. Rather, it is a symbol of His power and represents His control of things as a monarch's throne is a symbol of his power to rule. It indicates might or power and authority. He does not resemble His creatures in form; nor do any of His creatures resemble Him. The moment you can imagine what God is, He is not God. Having images of Jesus is incorrect, and, therefore, He cannot be God.[3]

Religion and its ideas were presented in paintings, drawings, sculptures, and architecture to express belief in a higher place of power. Art was a way of rearranging the mundane to make it seem celestial. It applied human creativity and ability to the ordinary to make it extraordinary and was a reminder of good, evil, life, and death.

During the fifteenth and sixteenth centuries, three new Muslim empires were founded: the Ottoman Turks in Asia Minor and Eastern Europe, the Safavids in Iran, and the Moghuls in India. These empires came to be renowned for their art and culture and were pioneers in the development of Islamic Art and Culture. Islamic Art encompassed miniature paintings, calligraphy, pottery and ceramics, carpets and textiles, jewellery, and architecture. Arabic calligraphy takes decades to master. It has always been considered an art form due to the elegant flow and meticulous formation of its letters.

Because my work is conceptual and nonrepresentational, people are able to interpret it in any desired sense. However, there is one vital aspect ubiquitous in all my art; an element of spirituality that forms the basis of every piece.

---

[2] Lindsay Farrell, Extract from, *The Hand of God in the Art of Michelangelo.*
[3] Dr Zakir Naik, *Concept of God in Major Religions.*

Spirituality and spiritual art have different connotations and yet share a commonality. Spirituality is a form of transition from the material world we live in to a level where greater subliminal things begin to matter and take precedence.

Art inspired by spiritual concepts has addressed humanity's most profound needs and life's greatest mysteries. Works of art can aid artists and viewers to achieve transcendence, the awareness of forces beyond the visible material world. Artists and viewers tend to look at art for contemplative, emotional, and revelatory experiences like those provided by religion. Spirituality and Art have been intertwined for decades, particularly in the work of American Abstract Expressionist Artists of the 1940s and 1950s, such as Wassily Kandinsky, Mark Rothko, and Barnett Newman, who have influenced my own paintings.

In their essay on Spirituality and Art, Jean Robertson and Craig McDaniel commented;
"The most powerful refuge of spiritual art in the 20th century was non-objective art. Some of the artists who were making abstract works were on a quest to see if art could inspire a transcendental state similar to the sublime feeling that nature could inspire. Abstract expressionist artists such as Wassily Kandinsky, Barnett Newman and Mark Rothko hoped viewers would experience a spiritual revelation, or at least a deeply meditative feeling, while gazing at abstract surfaces or forms".

In May 2007, Reverend Lone Jensen, an acclaimed pastor of Valley Unitarian Universalist Church in Arizona, gave a speech during which he stated;
"In what was then a quiet tree lined neighbourhood, I found the Rothko Chapel [Houston, Texas]. Outside is a reflecting pool with a "Broken Obelisk" dedicated to the Reverend Martin Luther King".
He felt as if he had embarked on a pilgrimage upon visiting the chapel and says;
"I liked Rothko, but these canvasses seemed at first to be entirely black and devoid of meaning. Still I had come a long way so I sat quietly and let my eyes adjust. Colours appeared slowly, browns and purples and reds, subtle shapes and shadows. I sat quietly. I looked at the centre of the floor where a single pillow had been left. And deep from within my soul an ancient grief arose. I began to cry and could not stop even as curious visitors passed by".

This is a great example of how Abstract Expressionist art seems to compel the viewer into a state of contemplation.

Stephen Polcari, an author on Abstract Expressionism, describes Barnett Newman's *Broken Obelisk* as consisting of a "pyramid topped by a reversed obelisk ascending yet torn, or broken at its top … In my opinion, the obelisk is a monolithic stature which represents the transcendence of the perceiver to another world, far beyond normal attainment and known to a few through the written sacred scriptures. The *Broken Obelisk* indicates the upward direction of this world, which is difficult to reach, with most people passing through life unable to do so – hence the break."

About this creation of his, Barnett Newman wrote, "the Obelisk is concerned with life and I hope that I have transformed its tragic content into a glimpse of the sublime. It is a chapel dedicated to all faith and in the foyer you find scriptures from all the major religions."

William Syrness, in *Contemplation for Protestants,* states;
"Much of modern art, I would say, does nothing to encourage real contemplation, that is, the active indwelling of forms and colours that spark our affection, even our love. But some artists did this more successfully than others, as in the case of Rothko and Newman. When this art is successful it moves the viewer toward a deeper contemplation of life, toward delight or dismay. When it is not, it leaves the viewer to examine the surface of things. The best art has always encouraged deep reflection, and people continue to respond to art of this kind. Indeed I believe many secular people find art important, precisely because it appeals to the contemplative side of their their lives".

I truly believe that when one views a piece of art, it is very much about the state of mind the person is in at that moment. Unless one knows the artist and about his or her work, the individual subconsciously interprets the work from the artist's perspective and state of mind.

Although art and religion go back a long way, art and science has been only recently interlinked. I was quite fascinated at the way Damien Hirst related art with faith and science. His exhibition, *titled New Religion*, inaugurated the gallery space inside a working Anglican Church and highlighted the conflict between science and religion.

"There are four important things in life: religion, love, art and science," Hirst once said. The result was a mixture of reinvented iconography in the form of silk-screen prints and sculptures. A large silk-screen print of a tablet cut into three equal sections depicted the holy scientific trinity: pathology, physiology, and pharmacology. Hirst felt that people's faith was moving away from God and religion to science and medicine. His work is a virtue of art that strives towards the revelation and expression of his philosophy of life. The art is not so spiritual in form but concerned more with the concepts of life and survival. One may not be in a meditative state while viewing a Hirst, but it's very much there and yet not. Like we are very much present on this earth, yet are rather oblivious about our existence. In this manner, Hirst attempts to utilise medicinal and scientific material to illustrate the relatively valid purposes of our lives. His philosophy of biological survival has similarities to the religion of Scientology, where survival, dealing with life situations, salvation, and rehabilitation are the main purposes of life.

Scientology is a religion created by L. Ron Hubbard in 1955, which deals with the human spirit and its relationship to the universe and its Creator. The basic message of life, according to Scientology, is survival across the Eight Dynamics: 1) self, 2) creativity, 3) group survival, 4) the human species, 5) life forms, 6) physical universe, 7) spiritual dynamics, and 8) existence as infinity. Scientology is not based on faith or trust in God but in achieving one's destiny by applying its principles.

Art and religion will continue to be entwined regardless of which context it is being expressed in, as in the case of Hirst. His philosophy and thought process is very different from mine, but there is definitely a religious connotation which is so special and meaningful, especially to those who have an interest in art and religion and are open-minded to the different interpretations by various artists – as long as they are respectful of each other's faiths.

However, there have been many disagreements about the world of art and religion. Art and religion, although coherent at times, continue to cross swords. For example, in 1989, Andres Serrano's *P– – – Christ* caused an absolute furore in New York. It was a painting of Jesus Christ submerged in the artist's urine. New York City mayor Rudy Giuliani banned it from being exhibited. Serrano, who was brought up as a Catholic, disrespected a prophet who was so special and is still the main spirit of Christianity, which millions of people worldwide follow and worship.

Seeing images of Jesus, which many Christians also refer to as God or the Lord, in forms of sculpture, paintings, and photographs is difficult for me to accept as a Muslim. One of the commandments of God is that "You must not make for yourself an idol of any kind, or an image of anything in the heavens or on the earth or in the sea" (Deuteronomy 5:8).

However, seeing artists disrespect Christ like this or make cartoons of Prophet Mohammed (PBUH) for their work of art in a blasphemous way simply abhors me. I do not believe this is either a form of freedom of speech or freedom of expression, not when you are disrespecting such revered prophets and know you are upsetting many fellow human beings for one's selfish gain.

Andrej Tisma is of a similar opinion: "this is what makes 'art' – anything that causes a rage, which makes headlines, that is 'cutting edge. Both religion and art lack spirituality and primary human innocence. A first hand conscience of the absolute and the meaning of existence have disappeared." Blasphemous art has saturated the art market over the past few decades, so it is no longer cutting edge.

I don't know whether I'm going to make headlines, but I'm trying to express the presence of God in my work with utmost respect to all religions and in reverence to the Almighty God.

CHAPTER 5
CIRCLE OF LIFE

I moved from the Saga Centre Studio, Ladbroke Grove, to a larger space at Linen House in Queen's Park. The decision to move again was a direct result of the success I achieved during the two solo exhibitions I had immediately after my MA Fine Art Degree show.

My first solo exhibition was sponsored by Lloyds TSB and held in their Private Banking office in Mayfair, London. It was the first time my paintings were for sale, and it was the most exciting time of my life. I was intrigued to see if people could relate to my work, if they could resonate with my work, and if they understood my thought process behind each piece. I was also curious to see how the viewers interpreted my work. What would they feel when they stood in front of my paintings?

I was pleasantly surprised at how well the work was received by such a mixed audience. Although I was not catering to a specific audience, I assumed that because there was such a strong presence of Quranic verses expressed in Arabic Kufic calligraphic form and the spiritual concept of my work, a larger Muslim audience would be drawn towards it. I was elated to be proved wrong as I witnessed people of all faiths drawn to my exhibition *titled Creation*. This series of paintings represented various aspects of God's creation of this planet in a non-representational form. Six months after this exhibition, I had another solo exhibition sponsored by ING Bank. And again, I was pleasantly surprised that my audience was very drawn to the application of this very stylised Arabic Kufic script within the overall composition of the painting.

However, the four years leading to my solo exhibition titled *Elements of Nature* in a commercial gallery were the most difficult and emotionally taxing years of my life. My paternal grandmother sadly passed away on 9th January 2007, and both my beloved parents soon followed.

I helped nurse my grandmother in my family home during the last few months of her life. Watching someone so very dear to me lose control of her life and become increasingly dependent on everyone around her made me realise that our lives do not belong to us but to The Almighty Allah. "Allah gives us life and unto Him is our return" (Quran, Surah Al-Baqara 2:28).

My grandmother was so full of life and zest, one of the most amazing, loving, and sociable human beings I have ever had the pleasure of knowing. I was truly honoured to be a part of her life and so close to her heart. "Meri Pyari" (My Love), as I lovingly called her, was a prominent figure throughout my childhood. She taught me many of the fundamental values of love, life, and Islam.

The day she passed away, I was working in my studio. My father, her only child, and my mother were with her during her last few moments. Mummy began to read one of the chapters from the Quran, Surah Yasin, referred to as the heart of the Quran, to my grandma, and as she finished the last verse, Grandma took her last breath.

This was a poignant moment for my parents as they had also been extremely close to her. Although I was devastated that I wasn't with my Grandma when she passed away, I felt at peace knowing she wasn't alone when she took her last breath and left this world; she spent her last day with her only child and beloved daughter-in-law.

When Grandma moved in with me three months prior to her death, I began playing the entire series of the Quran on a tape recorder so that she could listen to the words of Allah recited to her daily. She was an extremely pious and religious lady and had read chapters of the Quran daily throughout most of her life. Now that she was unable to do so, I thought she would enjoy listening to a recitation of it. I had instructed her carers to change and turn over the tapes when they ended. I'm not sure whether the tapes were repeatedly played or listened to more than once, but what I do know is the day Grandma took her last breath was the day the last tape of the Quran recitation played in the recorder, and the Quran was completed.

I will never know if instances such as this were coincidences, but my faith has taught me that when one is pious, religious, and God-fearing, God is there for them in times of need. I believe Allah was there for my grandmother during the most crucial time of her life and did not let her down. She passed away peacefully in the comfort of her own home, with her loved ones beside her. What more could a person ask for at such a poignant moment as when death takes over life, one is parted from loved ones, and the only life ever known transitions into the unknown?

As is said, "Death is a certainty; life isn't."

I went to the London Art Fair the weekend after Grandma passed away, as in Islam, we only mourn for three days. I happened to view a spot painting by Damien Hirst titled *Cineole*. It was a circular spot painting, with a diameter of approximately one metre and formed part of a three-painting series. One of them was a monochromatic painting, displaying different shades of grey; the other composed a myriad of soft pastel colours. I was immediately drawn to the painting hung in the middle of the two. *Cineole* was a spherical mix of bright, joyful colours and brought a smile to my face.

I wasn't aware then of the thoughts and concepts behind Damien Hirst's spot paintings. But what I knew was that to me, these paintings represented the circle of life.

I had witnessed the circle of life whilst taking care of my ailing grandmother. She was ninety-one years old when she sadly passed away and had reverted to the characteristics of an infant, needing to be bathed, dressed, fed, and cared for.

As infants, we are raised by our parents, who nurture us from the time of birth as we enter this world completely helpless and dependent. When we grow into adulthood, our parents are the ones rendered feeble and reliant by old age. I believe, it then becomes our responsibility to look after them the way they looked after us during childhood.

And your Lord has decreed that you worship none but Him. And you be dutiful to your parents. if one of them attain old age in your life, say not to them a word of disrespect, nor shout at them but address them in terms of honour. (Quran, 17:23)

And lower unto them the wing of submission and humanity through mercy, and say: "My Lord Bestow on them your Mercy as they did bring me up when I was young." (Quran, 17:24)

I felt lucky to have had the opportunity to care for my grandmother in her very fragile and sensitive state and to be her strength and support, the same way she had been mine as a child.

Every time I look at *Cineole* (which I have titled "Circle of Life"), which now hangs in my home in London, I smile at the colourful reminder of the wonderful relationship I had with my beloved grandmother.

Allah 1, oil on canvas, 2004, by Aisha Cahn.

CHAPTER 6
NAMES / CHARACTERISTICS OF GOD

In 2007, Ahmed Moustafa, a renowned Arabic calligrapher and artist born in Egypt, created a series of works featuring the cube. He discovered that a perfect cube consists of ninety-nine smaller cubes and built an installation on which he inscribed the ninety-nine Divine Names of Allah, demonstrating the perfection of God. He linked the cube to structural and fractural geometry in which the individual unit is a small replica of the whole. He states, "Just as diversity of nature is unceasingly testifying the Oneness of its Creator and His limitless attributes, man came to realise that the structure of the smallest detail in the vast natural world always conforms to the structure of the whole."

This inspired me to do a series on the ninety-nine Names of Allah, which formed part of my first commercial solo exhibition at the Albemarle Gallery in Mayfair, London, in April 2011. The exhibition was titled *Elements of Nature*. I spent twenty months creating an entirely new body of work for this exhibition.

The elements of nature that formed the essence of my exhibition were fourfold: wind/air, water, earth, and fire. Without these elements, as I note, the world could not function in the perfect and orderly fashion that it does for humans to survive on this planet.

Yet, as I also note, my observations also involved humankind's placement on earth. Through reflection, I realised that one creates divisions wherever he or she is in this world – divisions of boundaries, countries, cultures, creeds, race, wealth, and power.

To each of you We have ordained a code of law and a way of life. If Allah had willed, He would have made you one nation, but His Will is to try you with what He has given each of you. So strive with one another in doing good. To Allah you will all return, then He will inform you of the truth regarding your differences. (Quran 5:48)

My interpretation of this verse is that we could have all been one colour, one race, one creed, and one community. But God created humankind to form different cultures and communities for us to live in harmony with each other rather than in conflict and creating divisions amongst each other.

I wanted to express this observation within the series *Elements of Nature*. To symbolise these divisions was going to be challenging. Whenever I begin a new series of work, the most difficult thing to do is to get started with a new source of inspiration. I never know when, what, or how this will take place. What is so amazing is that this new form of inspiration just happens. Something within my inner self triggers an emotion or I may have an obscure vision, and that will be the initial source of the message I am trying to convey through my work. This leads me to search for an aesthetic source of inspiration to be inspired by. An example of this was when I contemplated over a cup of coffee at a coffee shop of how I should incorporate humankind creating division on this planet for my next exhibition. As I sipped my coffee, I looked around. I was in a very contemplative mood that day, and all I could see around me were buildings, one after another, because of the metropolis I live in.

My realisation of this urban metropolis, led me to observe the surroundings of architectural structures which create divisions and boundaries. My mind then went on to looking at the architecture of these buildings, which were of various designs and constructions. The penny had dropped, and I now found myself with a big smile on my face. I had discovered the source of inspiration for my next series of work was going to be through architectural forms.

At the same time, the series is also a quest for unity. In my paintings, I hope to bring to light the similarities between science and all the world's religions – in particular, the links between the three Abrahamic religions: Judaism, Christianity, and Islam.

Many layers of inspiration, thoughts, painterly techniques, and processes went into creating works for *Elements of Nature*. However, the road to completion was difficult and poignant for reasons other than artistic complexities. My mother was terminally ill, suffering from ovarian cancer.

Mummy used to be Dad's carer as he had suffered a long history of Emphysema and was admitted to the ICU at the Royal Brompton Hospital several times. The family was prepared to grieve for Dad passing away when the time came. What we weren't prepared for was our precious mother being diagnosed with ovarian cancer in November 2008 and then sadly passing away and leaving us forever thirteen months later, in December 2009.

Mummy was an incredibly strong, disciplined, and virtuous human being. She was a very pious person, who followed her faith by the book, without bending rules or changing practices to suit her convenience, as most of us do.

When she was in the North London Hospice, I visited her every day and had afternoon tea with her. It was our time together; just my mother and me, one on one, such quality time spent together. Although I had a very close relationship with my mother, this time spent together was so precious. It put so many things in perspective.

When Mummy was told of her poor prognosis, she was, of course, very saddened. But she realised there was no point in being depressed about it, and she just embraced it. Seeing this positive attitude inspired me so much.

"We all have to die at some point. However, none of us know where, when, or how we are going to die. Isn't it better to take control, of one's life and death? By taking control of one's affairs, by having the opportunity to say goodbye to all our loved ones by leaving a legacy, by reflecting on one's life, and leaving this life with a clear conscience, and a light heart. Most of all, by realising that one is going to the unknown and coming to terms with the fact that there is something far more powerful and superior than us mortal beings, which most of us term as "God". Surely, it is a blessing to know that I have a little time to do all this."
These were some of my mother's words during the initial stage of her poor prognosis.
It was the most uplifting and spiritual time of my life, being with someone so very special and dear to me. To have this positive attitude towards death, knowing that you are going to leave this material world and one's loved ones, to go to the unknown, was just so inspiring. None of us really think about death, yet it is an absolute certainty.

One evening as I sat with Mummy, I could sense that she wasn't going to live much longer, and this would be her last weekend with us. "I saw the angels last night. I saw my mother, my father, and my brother and sister." These were some of the last words Mummy said to me the day before she passed away.

As Mummy said these words to me, I had a fleeting thought: *All Mummy is waiting for is for death to take her away. Is this how I would like to die?*

I never thought more about this until six months later, when two very dear friends and my first cousin had sudden deaths. They all left behind so many unattended situations and unresolved affairs. They did not even have the chance to say goodbye to their loved ones.

Mummy's prayers and her inner strength helped her through those last few months of her life. She took control of her life and death and dealt with everything she needed to before she passed away. She bequeathed whatever she wanted to, to whom she wanted to whilst she was alive. She felt life was too short for any animosity and united friends and family. Mummy also asked for forgiveness from everyone who came to see her, as she felt that subconsciously, we all may say and do things which could offend or hurt someone. In a nutshell, Mummy tried to leave this world with no stone unturned and with a clear heart and a pure soul. She was a very spiritual lady and concerned about her fellow human beings.

I began to wonder whether it is preferable to experience a slow and peaceful death or a quick and sudden one. When people are taken from this world suddenly and unexpectedly, there are so many matters left unresolved and moments of regret that remain because there was no opportunity to make amends or even to say goodbye. If I had control over my death, I know which manner of death I would choose, God willing, as only He knows best.

One afternoon during the last week of Mummy's life, she told me she would like to die between the prayer times of Asr (late afternoon) and Maghreb (sunset) on a Thursday. I asked Mummy why, to which she replied, "Asr is the end of the day for Muslims, and Maghreb is the beginning of the next day and being Friday (Jummah), this day every week is as important to the Muslims as Sunday is to the Christians and Saturday is to the Jews."

When my mother took her last breath, I was the only one with her. Her hand clenched mine. There was silence and then a sudden breath in three short intervals. During this time, I found myself very emotional and repeatedly said in a soft, gentle voice, "There is no God but Allah. Glory be to Allah. Praise be to Allah, and Allah is Great" Mummy was leaving this world and going to the unknown. She was going to be with her Lord, the One who gave her life and was now taking it away from her.

I telephoned my father immediately to give him this sad news. In the background, I heard the call for prayer for the Maghreb prayer time as it was now 3:45 on Thursday, 10th December 2009, the end of one day and the beginning of the next, Friday. If Mummy had wished for anything else during this time, I am sure it would have been granted to her. Not many of us have the opportunity to take control of our deaths, and in Mummy's case, the precise timing of it. May God rest her soul in peace, forgive her of any sins, and grant her a place in heaven. Inshallah.

God works in very mysterious ways. I hadn't been there when my grandmother passed away and found it very difficult to deal with this. However, I had taken great pains to mentally prepare myself and come to terms with the fact that I might not be there when Mummy took her last breath. But it just so happened that I was the only one with her.

My Arabic teacher told me after my grandmother passed away that it is up to the deceased to decide who they want next to him or her in the last moments of their life. God grants this final wish.

Mummy was extremely interested in my artwork. She believed it was my way of reaching out to the world and sharing my own beliefs and knowledge of the Oneness of God. During my visits to the hospice, I had taken my sketchbook along with me and worked in it whenever Mummy took short naps. These sketches turned out to be the initial stages of work for the installation of the *99 Names* of Allah for the exhibition *Elements of Nature*.

Judaism and Christianity have seventy-two names for God. In Islam, there are ninety-nine names for God; These names include characteristics/attributes of God: The Compassionate, The Forgiver, The Protector, The the Judge, The Creator, The Evolver, The Mighty, The Strong, and The Everlasting.

Ironically, when Mummy took her last and final breaths of her life, the two names of Allah that I had just finished sketching were 'The Compeller and The Mighty. Only an incredibly mighty and compelling source of power can take life from a human being. This source of power can only be that of the Almighty Creator of the heavens and the earth and all that is between them.

I continued working in my sketchbook on the 99 Names of Allah until I completed them. I then began translating the work onto canvasses, which I had painted in the various colours of the elements of nature. I finished the installation in December 2010, exactly a year after Mummy's death.

I displayed the ninety-nine canvasses on the four walls of the gallery space. This array of display was very important to me as when one thinks about the attributes of God, some of them are also fundamental characteristics of human beings. For example, we should also be more forgiving, more compassionate, more loving, more caring, more concealing, and more protective as human beings and towards our fellow human beings. Therefore, when the viewer is within the four walls of the gallery space, he or she can resonate with these attributes of God as they are coveted aspirations.

The 99 names/attributes of Allah: **The Compassionate, The Merciful, The Sovereign Lord, The Holy, The Source of Peace, The Guarantor, The Protector, The Compeller, The Most High, The Creator, The Rightful, The Fashioner of Forms, The Forgiving, The Subduer, The Bestower, The Provider, The Opener, The All Knowing, The Restrainer, The Expander, The Abaser, The Exalter, The Giver of Honour, The Giver of Dishonour, The All Hearing, The All Seer, The Judge, The Just, The Gentle, The All Aware, The Forbearing, The Magnificent, The All Forgiving, The Grateful, The Sublime, The Great, The Preserver, The Nourisher, The Bringer of Judgement, The Majestic, The Generous, The Watchful, The Responsive, The Omnipresent, The Wise, The Loving, The Glorious, The Resurrector, The Witness, The Truth, The Trustee, The Strong, The Firm, The Protecting Friend, The Praiseworthy, The Accounter, The Originator, The Restorer, The Giver of Life, The Bringer of Death, The Ever Living, The Self Existing, The Finder, The Magnificent, The One, The Unity, The Eternal, The Omnipotent, The Dominant, The Expediter, The Delayer, The First, The Last, The Manifest, The Hidden, The Protecting Friend, The Exalted, The Doer of Good, The Accepter of Repentance, The Avenger, The Pardoner, The Kind, The Owner of Sovereignty, The Lord of Majesty and Generosity, The Equitable, The Gatherer, The Rich, The Enricher, The Withholder, The Distresser, The Source of Good, The Light, The Guide, The Incomparable, The Everlasting, The Heir, The Guide to the Right Path, and The Patient.**

I miss my mother terribly. She carried me in her womb for nine months, she gave birth to me, she nurtured me, and she brought me up with some fine religious and moral values, which are the foundations of who I am today. I could not thank her enough for being such a wonderful mother. I believe she brought my siblings and me up to the best of her ability, and as long as I am alive, she will very much be a part of me. She would have been so elated to see what I accomplished with my knowledge of faith and spirituality and how I shared this knowledge with my fellow human beings through my work of art.

99 Names of Allah, at the Albemarle Exhibition, 2011, by Aisha Cahn.

The largest painting of the series is titled *Allah – The Creator of the Heavens and the Earth*. It has a perspex hemisphere over the name Allah. When viewing this piece, one can see his or her reflection in the hemisphere, with Allah's name radiating through it. This form of luminosity enables the viewer to resonate with the painting in a very contemplative manner because all of us have God's spirit within us, and the viewer's reflection almost enhances this.

Allah - The Creator of the Heavens and the Earth, oil on canvas, 2010, by Aisha Cahn.

CHAPTER 7
Void in My Life / Purpose of Life

After my mother passed away, Dad wanted to know more about my work. He showed a real interest towards it and wanted to get more involved with it. At times when I visited him, I took my sketchbook along to show him the latest series of paintings I was working on or photographs of the development and processes of the *Elements of Nature* series. Dad was particularly interested in the installation of the *99 Names of Allah*. He followed the entire process with me; from writing the names in Arabic in my sketchbook, to the various techniques I applied to the canvasses, and eventually, the final application of the perspex hemispheres to each canvas.

Dad was so excited about my first solo exhibition in a commercial art gallery, and he couldn't wait to see it. He had been in and out of hospital three times since January 2011 and was admitted again during the week of the exhibition launch. He insisted on being discharged from the hospital in time to attend the private viewing on Saturday, 2nd April 2011. I went to see him the day before and spent the entire afternoon and evening with him. We had an amazing day together, and he was in such good spirits. He asked me to pick out an outfit for him to wear to the Private View of my exhibition. Dad referred to me as his personal stylist due to my previous career as a fashion designer.

Dad had a bad start to the day on Saturday. Emergency doctors were called to his apartment, and paramedics insisted that he should go back to the hospital. He was so keen on coming to my show that he told all the medics about it and insisted that he must attend.

I knew he wasn't well enough to come to the show, but I didn't realise that twenty-four hours later, I would no longer have a father in my life. Although Dad hadn't been well, and his condition was deteriorating, I wasn't prepared for the sudden exit of his presence from my life, and it came as a huge shock to all of us. Although my father never made it to my show, I knew it meant a lot for him to be there. He had been with me throughout this incredible journey of creating two years of work. In spirit, I knew he was there.

Having lost my grandmother, mother, and father within four years, I felt as if an entire generation of my family had abruptly been wiped away from my life. I had been so very close to each of them; I had a special relationship and bond with each of these very important people in my life.

For the first time in my life, I felt a vast void and emptiness within myself. I suppose because their love was unconditional and due to their age, they didn't have a very active social life, so we spoke to each other several times a day. I knew they were always there for me any time of the day or night.

All of them had needed me in one way or another as they were helpless with their illnesses. I had tried to make sure I was there for them as much as possible. After they passed away, I felt unneeded and didn't have anyone to care for anymore. Even though I have two lovely daughters, we are all very independent and keep busy with our own lives.

I was at an extremely strange place in my life, especially after Dad passed away, and at a very low point within myself. When Grandma passed away, I still had Mummy and Dad and when Mummy passed away, I still had Dad. But when Dad passed away so suddenly, I found myself with nothing but emptiness around me. I lost that unconditional love and affection each of them showered upon me.

At this point in my life, I couldn't even go to the studio to paint. I was unable to concentrate and focus on work, and I felt completely uninspired. All I could think about was the loss of these three beloved family members.

In the Islamic tradition, when a close member of the family dies, only immediate family can bathe the body and prepare the person for the coffin and funeral. I was present at both my mother's and grandmother's funeral preparation. As my grandmother's funeral was the first one I had experienced, it was a very emotional and poignant moment for me, my sisters, my daughters, and nieces. Once there was life in this body, and now, Grandma was oblivious of the ritual taking place and to her body. Her soul was far removed from her body the day she took her last breath. "God gives us life and unto Him is our return."

We wrapped her body in a white cotton shroud that went around her layer after layer, ensuring none of her flesh was exposed except her beautiful face. We then placed her into the coffin and prepared her for the funeral ceremony. I remember thinking at the time that Grandma was taking nothing material away with her. Not even a speck of dust. The only things she was taking with her were her karma, her deeds, her remembrance, and her gratitude and appreciation to her Creator, her Lord, the Almighty God.

I went through the same emotional ritual of preparing for my mother's funeral, which again was very emotional. I remember thinking, *This is my mother lying here. She gave birth, life, to me, and now there is no more life in her. She is completely oblivious to everything around her.*

However, for my father's funeral preparation, my brother and other close male members of the family followed the same ritual. I saw my father lying in his coffin, wrapped in the purest of white cotton shroud and realising this really was the last of my loving parental generation. There was no more of my amazing grandmother, my beautiful mother, and my handsome father. Having experienced this three times in four years really makes you question the purpose of life.

The Gul Amin Residence, Wazirabad, Pakistan, and some of its orphan students.
A Project by Muslim Hands UK

CHAPTER 8
SELF-OBSESSION

As humans, we spend all our time in this world acquiring material things and attempting to gain status, wealth, and power. Whether we can acquire this or not, we still spend all our time striving and aspiring for this material gain. Yet, none of it comes with us when we leave this world and go to the unknown world. All we take with us are our deeds and karma. What truly matters after we die is how much time we dedicated in life towards worshipping God and thanking Him for creating this beautiful world for us to live in, how much we cared for our fellow human beings, and how much time we spent on ourselves to ensure the acquisition of humility, humbleness, and piety. What preparations have we made towards our deaths as we are all accountable for our good and bad deeds, which we will be either rewarded for or punished.

The only thing I have to give to my friends and family is love and affection; this is the way I was raised. I have friends from all walks of life, of different creeds and cultures, various age groups and social standings. However, the one commonality they all possess is a warm heart. It's the heart that makes you the person you are, not the mind. Love, affection, and emotions all stem from the heart. The heart is where the love for God lies. If you love someone, in effect, you love God. And if you hurt someone, in effect, you hurt God. We are all God's creation, so we should all be very mindful and considerate of our fellow human beings. If we hurt each other, we are really hurting God.

Now, the mind has a different function altogether. It tells us what we should and shouldn't do. Most of the time, we listen to it, act according to its instructions, and take responsibility for our actions. The mind is where the ego is, and if we only listen to the mind and not the heart, we can become very egotistical. That can become a very arrogant trait.

Sadhguru Jaggi Vasudev is an Indian yogi, mystic, poet. He said;
"Today in the world, we need to bring about a simple sense – a life sense. Right now, people only have ego sense, they have no life sense. They are ego sensitive, not life sensitive. When you are like this, you only see yourself as life, no one else is life. You can trample upon anything and anyone. But if you are life sensitive, everything is life in your experience, so you naturally behave very

sensibly with every other life around you. The ego will no longer be a problem if you become life sensitive".

Unfortunately, we have developed into a nation of self-obsession, focussed on power, control, and greed. A race of people for which everything is centred on us as individuals – our lives, our wants, and our desires. We live in a time of obscene consumerism, greed for power, and self-obsession. We have forgotten the remembrance of God and appreciation of existence. If only human beings could realise that we are what we are and have what we have only with the permission and will of God.

It is through my deep losses that I became conscious about the concept of self-obsession. I thought long and hard as to how I could ensure that my life does not revolve around me anymore and to focus on the acquisition of good deeds and looking after others. Hence, this is a journey from me to you, my fellow human beings.

I attempted to turn my life around and dedicate my time to matters more important than my own. In 2008, I set up the Aisha Cahn Foundation for the provision of direct aid to the poor and needy.

I wanted my first philanthropic project to be the setting up of an orphanage, which I managed to achieve in June 2011 in Wazirabad, Pakistan. The reasoning behind this is that in all three sacred scriptures, God has spoken about kindness to the orphans, to be fair to the orphans, to care for them, and to ensure their inheritance and belongings are looked after. Three of the main messengers were bereft of parents throughout their lives. Moses never saw his father after he was only three months old, Jesus did not have a father, and Prophet Mohammad (PBUH) was orphaned at the age of six. Hence, I had an absolute yearning to set up an orphanage because I believe there is nothing worse in this world than for a child to be unsheltered and without the love and vital guidance of parents.

All of us must face death at some stage in our lives, though we do not know when our time will come. People may believe that we are likely to be closer to death at an older age, rather than in youthful prime. However, one can never know. I know of so many people who are hale and hearty and have died suddenly, through no rhyme or reason.

As one can never know when death is coming, one should always be prepared for it. A classic example of an illness where we can prepare ourselves for death and, to some extent, even take control of our death is the terminal illness of cancer. As I lost my mother to cancer and watched how she took control of her life and death during her poor prognosis, I wanted to find out more about this terminal illness that took my mother from me.

It was a subject no one really wanted to talk about. It was this big C word that shouldn't be talked about as everyone feared it, including me. They feared it because of the poor prognosis cancer often has which ultimately leads to death. My mother enlightened me to an alternative perspective on two very sensitive and scary topics –cancer and death.

I wanted to have an exhibition to share this very personal experience with my mother. But I didn't know where to begin and how I was going to contextualise this in a positive light to so many people affected by cancer. It was going to be an exhibition inspired by the science of cells. It would also be a journey of expressionism, optimism, sadness, and knowledge that, I wanted to share with the world and through my art.

I embarked upon educating myself about the science of cells, in particular cancer cells. I spent time at the UCL laboratories at the Royal Free Hospital, at Cancer Research UK, and Imperial College, all of whom are making incredible progress in finding a cure for cancer through drug development and immunotherapy.

However, I was drawn more towards the immunology aspect for finding a cure for cancer and worked very closely with the professors at the Royal Free Hospital. I was in awe of the discovery that T cells and NK cells can destroy cancer. This breakthrough discovery sent me towards my initial source of inspiration, and I made further enquiries to understand NK cells, T cells, cancer cells, normal human cells, and stem cells.

All this research inspired me to create a series of work combining various media – including paintings, silk-screen prints, drawings, and three installations – for my exhibition *titled Embrace* at the Saatchi Gallery.

What was really interesting was that from the initial source of inspiration to the final layer of paint on the canvas, I continued to explore the theme of art and science, which has been a common thread throughout my work.

The reason for me sharing this very poignant experience of my life through my art is to show the positive side of when a cancer patient is given a poor prognosis. One has time to take control of one's life and death and do whatever needs to be done or said before leaving this world. I wanted to have an exhibition conveying this positive holistic approach to cancer, dedicated to my beautiful mother for her positive attitude towards her poor prognosis and towards death.

Installation of 325 acrylic discs, oil painted 2016, by Aisha Cahn for
the exhibition titled *Embrace* at the Saatchi Gallery.

As a Muslim, I believe preparation for death involves belief in The One God; The Four Sacred Scriptures – The Quran, The Bible, The Torah, and The Psalms; The Angels; and Believe in all of God's Prophets and Messengers; God's Predestination; and The Hereafter. It also includes following the Ten Commandments, the fundamentals of leading a good and pious life, and most importantly being considerate to our fellow human beings. This is just my belief, and I am sure many people have their own ways of preparing and dealing with death according to their faith and beliefs. All of this can only hold relevance if one has faith.

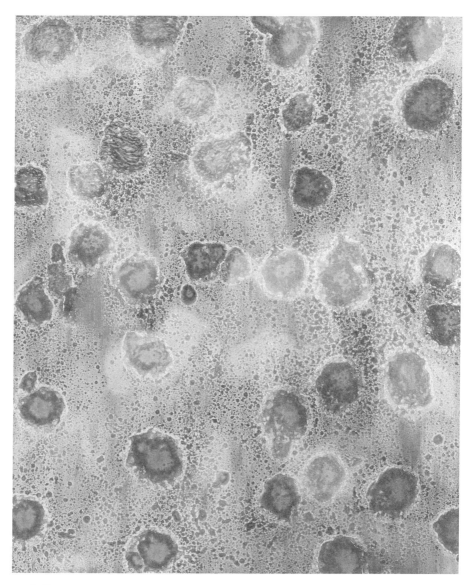

Celloplane 4, oil and mixed media on canvas, 2014, by Aisha Cahn.

We are born with an intelligence which enables us to discover and appreciate all of God's incredible creations and differentiate between right and wrong. We are not answerable to anyone in this world except to the One and only Almighty God, so we cannot be judgemental. We have freedom of choice and free will. We choose to either be guided or not. We are, therefore, solely responsible for our actions and must bear the consequences. Irrespective of our choices, it is God we ask for forgiveness, and to Him, we repent.

We have a direct connection to Him through our prayers. This is the beauty of our Creator. God did not simply create man, give him life, and banish him to earth, expecting him to have complete knowledge of everything. Instead, He provided a series of manuals and instructions to act as guidance throughout life. These manuals are the sacred scriptures which were revealed to humankind by way of revelations conveyed by God through the Angel Gabriel to the chosen Prophets and Messengers. The Prophet David (PBUH) was given The Psalms of David, Moses (PBUH) received The Torah, and The Bible was revealed to Jesus (PBUH). The final and historically unchanged Holy Book, The Quran, was bestowed to the last Prophet of Islam, Mohammed (PBUH). The revelations were written on various materials as the messages were revealed to the messengers. They were documented on parchment, fabric, leaves, animal skin, and stone. When the messengers passed away, their disciples compiled these messages into forms of sacred scriptures.

God sent these Prophets and Messengers when He felt people needed to be reminded there is only One God, and He created the universe, the planets, the stars, the entire galaxies, and every living creature on this planet.

Recently, a lady walked into my studio, wanting a favour. I had seen her around the building a few times, but we had never spoken. On entering the room, she noticed my paintings on the walls and immediately recognised the spiritual elements within them. We embarked on a conversation about art, spirituality, religion, science, and the creation of the universe. As she listened to me speak about my faith in God and the three Abrahamic religions, she admitted to feeling envious that I held such strong beliefs as she had never experienced anything similar. She had spent her life wanting everything to be tangible and material and searching for proof of everything. She didn't practice her religion or believe in God. Her conviction lay in the idea that she was in absolute control of her own life. I relayed to her that to a certain extent, one does create one's destiny apart from the four preordained destinies – birth, death, health, and wealth – which no one has control over.

After listening to the preordained destinies, she shook her head. She was adamant that she would control her death. She planned to travel to Switzerland to get herself euthanised to "die with dignity." I attempted to explain she could perchance die a sudden death as we stood speaking, without any warning or explanation, and there would be nothing she could do about it. She left the studio with a hint of doubt in her mind about her way of thinking. I was pleased to have opened her up to an idea, she had been closed to probably her entire life.

This lady believed that anyone with a belief in God or faith in religion possessed such conviction as a way of retaining a crutch, something to hold onto to give one support. I had never heard anything so paradoxical before. Personally, my belief in God and faith has given me so much freedom. Leaning on a crutch hinders one; one is dependent and physically restricted. I, on the other hand, have not felt lost, confused, or laden with worries of the unknown. I feel my faith has kept my mind open and grounded in order to let my soul be free. It is my choice how I use this freedom. I can either focus on becoming a good human being or become a self-obsessed one. The choice is mine. One can transgress from the guidance of the Holy Scriptures or abide by them and take advantage of the guidance God has provided.

Creation, mixed media on canvas, 2005, 9 x 40x40 cms, by Aisha Cahn

CHAPTER 9
TRUST IN GOD

Trusting God is a very powerful yet subservient thing to do. It doesn't mean people have no control over their actions, deeds, or decisions. On the contrary, they take full responsibility for the choices made, but they turn to God for guidance and reassurance to help them make the right decision.

I have turned to God for guidance when I have found myself in a dilemma and needed to make some major decisions after spending days pondering the ifs, whats, whens, whys, and hows relating to the huge decisions that I need to make.

In Islam, there is a special prayer called Istekhara. One only performs this prayer when unsure about making a major decision. The person asks family and friends for advice, but at the end of the day, the decision maker is responsible for its outcome. However, by doing the Istekhara prayer, one puts trust in God, asking Him for guidance and for help in making the right decision. Basically, this is the intention of the prayer: " Our Lord, my intention for this Istekhara prayer is for you to guide and help me make the right decision for (whatever the dilemma). I put my trust in You and know that whatever the outcome will be, it will be the right one."

Whenever I perform the Istekhara prayer and step away from my prayer mat, I feel like a whole burden has been lifted from my head. I no longer find myself pondering over if, what, when, why, how, and so on. I continue working towards making the decision, and God steers me towards making the right one. There are many layers of events that unfold before the decision is made. This decision may not necessarily be the one I believe I would have made on my own or even to have a positive result. But because I put my utmost trust in God, I know it to be the right decision.

I had to make the biggest decision in my life recently, and most people would not have acted in the manner that I did. It was an emotionally distressing and a life-changing decision which involved the closest members of my family. I thought hard and deeply about my choices, actions, and ultimately my decision. My whole perception of life changed during this very emotional time, in the sense that life changed so dramatically from one day to the next. I never fully realised all the consequences I would be faced with.

People change, life changes, circumstances change, people evolve, and life is continuously evolving. Hence, when one is faced with such uncertain times, it's important to be in control of oneself. I was able to take control from my inner self, as it was from here that I got my inner strength and confidence to help me embark on the next chapter of my life.

The beauty of life is that when we wake up every morning, we embark on a brand-new day. No one has lived or experienced that day before you. No one knows what is in store for all of us from one day to the next. Each new day we must deal with excitement, surprises, sorrow, and pain.

In my experience, there is only one way to deal with life, and that is with utmost positivity and gratitude to God. Even if one is going through pain and hardship. "Verily after every hardship there is ease, verily after every hardship there is ease" (Quran 94:6).

I know this because I put my total trust in God through the Istekhara prayer, and He steered me towards this life-changing decision. Due to this, my whole perspective of life changed. It changed in a way that created such a positive mental attitude in everything I said and did moving forward. Every day I prayed and asked God to give me inner strength, courage, and confidence to help me deal with this decision.

My mother (bless her, and may her soul always rest in peace) once said to me, "If you remember God when times are good for you, He will always be there for you in times of need." How true is this, and how right was my beautiful mother! God was there for me during my time of need. He gave me the care, love, and support of my beautiful daughters, Jemma-Lia and Hanah; my housekeeper, Marilyn; my chauffeur, Stephen; and my family and friends to help me through this change.

God is the Almighty, the All Knower, and I truly believe He knew why I needed to embark on a new journey and a new chapter in my life. I also believe that He took me from darkness and brought me into light.

It really is quite simple. If you are a believer, place your trust in God, and remember, united we stand, and divided we fall.

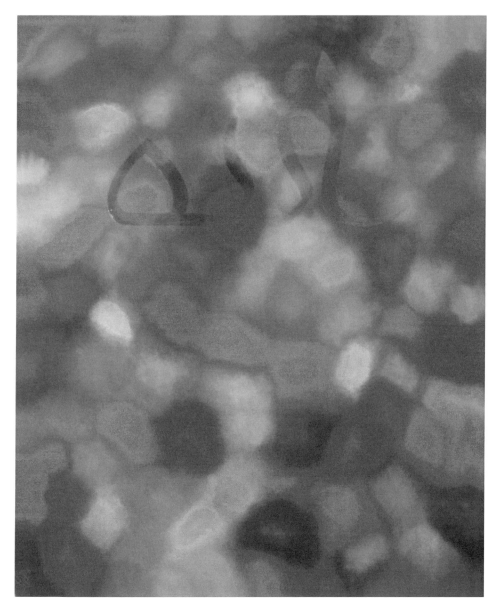

Unity, oil on canvas 2010, by Aisha Cahn.

ABOUT THE AUTHOR

Aisha Cahn is a British contemporary artist whose work reveals her deep spirituality and philosophical nature. She has become very concerned about the divisions humankind creates for itself. Through her work, she tries to reconcile these divisions by uniting the disciplines of faith and science in a form of contemporary spiritual art. It is this form of spirituality that has made her appreciate the genesis of things and to become more philanthropic as she focuses on the less fortunate and the needy.

She has had many group shows and six solo shows since 2007. She was an undergraduate at London College of Fashion in Fashion Design, a postgraduate at Central St Martins College of Art and Design in Fine Art, a Lecturer at LCF, Chair of the Development Council for the University of the Arts London, and is now a Trustee of the Court of Governors for the UAL. Cahn is an Ambassador for Muslim Hands UK and has fulfilled many philanthropic projects through the Aisha Cahn Foundation.

Lightning Source UK Ltd.
Milton Keynes UK
UKRC02n0100050618
323731UK00002B/43

9 781504 395380